EMMANUEL JOSEPH

Shaping Success: Post-Job Loss

Copyright © 2025 by Emmanuel Joseph

All rights reserved. No part of this publication may be reproduced, stored or transmitted in any form or by any means, electronic, mechanical, photocopying, recording, scanning, or otherwise without written permission from the publisher. It is illegal to copy this book, post it to a website, or distribute it by any other means without permission.

First edition

*This book was professionally typeset on Reedsy.
Find out more at reedsy.com*

Contents

1	Chapter 1: The Unexpected Turn	1
2	Chapter 2: Embracing the Change	3
3	Chapter 3: Self-Reflection and Reassessment	5
4	Chapter 4: Skill Development and Lifelong Learning	7
5	Chapter 5: Networking and Building Connections	9
6	Chapter 6: Crafting a Winning Resume and Cover Letter	11
7	Chapter 7: Mastering the Job Interview	13
8	Chapter 8: Exploring Alternative Career Paths	15
9	Chapter 9: Financial Management During Transition	17
10	Chapter 10: Mental and Emotional Well-being	19
11	Chapter 11: Staying Motivated and Persistent	21
12	Chapter 12: Celebrating Success and Moving Forward	23

1

Chapter 1: The Unexpected Turn

The sudden jolt of job loss can feel like the ground shifting beneath one's feet. Initially, there is disbelief, a sense of unreality that engulfs the mind. The emotions that follow—fear, sadness, anger—create a whirlwind, leaving one feeling helpless. It's easy to internalize the job loss as a reflection of personal failure, rather than an external circumstance beyond control. However, it is critical to recognize that this unexpected turn is not the end of the road, but rather a redirection. Embracing this shift with a positive mindset can open doors to new opportunities and personal growth that were previously unseen.

Coming to terms with the job loss involves acknowledging the pain and confusion it brings. It is a natural response to grieve for the stability and identity tied to the lost job. Allowing oneself to process these emotions is a crucial step towards healing. It is equally important to shift focus from the loss to the possibilities that lie ahead. This redirection of energy can spark new interests and lead to unforeseen paths that bring fulfillment and success.

Understanding that job loss is a common experience can provide some solace. Countless individuals have faced similar challenges and emerged stronger. These stories of resilience serve as a reminder that setbacks are temporary and can be transformed into stepping stones. By learning from these examples, one can find inspiration and strength to navigate through the uncertainty.

Support systems play a pivotal role during this transition. Friends, family, and professional networks can offer emotional support, practical advice, and even job leads. Engaging with these networks can alleviate feelings of isolation and provide a sense of community. It is important to reach out, share experiences, and seek help when needed. The collective wisdom and encouragement from others can be a powerful source of motivation and guidance.

The key to overcoming job loss lies in maintaining a positive outlook and being open to change. Instead of dwelling on what has been lost, focus on what can be gained. This mindset shift can transform the experience from a crisis into an opportunity for reinvention. With determination and a proactive approach, the journey from job loss to success becomes not only possible but also deeply rewarding.

2

Chapter 2: Embracing the Change

Change, especially when unexpected, can be daunting. Job loss forces a reevaluation of one's life and career, pushing individuals out of their comfort zones. However, embracing change is essential for growth. Viewing job loss not as a failure but as an opportunity for transformation can lead to remarkable outcomes. It requires a shift in perspective, from fear to curiosity, and from resignation to determination.

The first step in embracing change is accepting the reality of the situation. Denial and resistance only prolong the suffering. By acknowledging the job loss and its impact, one can begin to move forward. This acceptance does not mean giving up; rather, it means letting go of what was and opening up to what could be. It is an act of courage and a necessary foundation for rebuilding.

Once acceptance is in place, it is time to explore new possibilities. This can be an exciting phase of discovery. Reflecting on past experiences, identifying passions, and considering new career paths can spark a sense of adventure. It is an opportunity to rediscover oneself and align one's career with personal values and interests. This process of self-discovery can lead to a more fulfilling and meaningful professional life.

During this transition, setting realistic goals is crucial. Ambitious yet attainable objectives provide direction and motivation. Breaking down larger goals into smaller, manageable steps can prevent overwhelm and create a sense of progress. Celebrating small victories along the way reinforces positive momentum and builds confidence. It is important to stay patient and persistent, understanding that meaningful change takes time.

Support and guidance from mentors, career coaches, or support groups can be invaluable during this period. These resources offer insights, encouragement, and practical advice. They can help navigate the challenges of change and provide accountability. Engaging with a supportive community fosters a sense of belonging and reminds individuals that they are not alone in their journey. Embracing change, with the right mindset and support, can lead to unprecedented personal and professional growth.

3

Chapter 3: Self-Reflection and Reassessment

Job loss presents a unique opportunity for deep self-reflection. It is a time to pause and reassess one's life, career, and aspirations. This introspection is crucial for understanding one's strengths, weaknesses, and true passions. It provides clarity and direction for the next steps, ensuring that future endeavors are aligned with personal values and long-term goals.

The process of self-reflection begins with an honest evaluation of past experiences. Identifying accomplishments, challenges, and learning moments provides valuable insights. Reflecting on what worked well and what didn't helps in recognizing patterns and preferences. This awareness is essential for making informed decisions about the future. It also highlights areas for improvement and skill development.

Reassessing one's career involves exploring new possibilities. It is an opportunity to consider different industries, roles, and work environments. Researching various career options and conducting informational interviews can provide a broader perspective. This exploration helps in identifying potential paths that align with one's interests and strengths. It opens up avenues that may have been previously overlooked.

Aligning career goals with personal values is critical for long-term satisfaction. Understanding what truly matters—whether it's work-life balance, social impact, creativity, or financial stability—guides the decision-making process. This alignment ensures that career choices are not only financially rewarding but also personally fulfilling. It leads to a more authentic and purpose-driven professional life.

Creating a personal development plan is the next step. This plan outlines specific goals, strategies, and timelines for achieving them. It includes skill development, networking, and job search activities. Having a clear plan provides structure and focus, making the transition smoother. Regularly reviewing and adjusting the plan ensures that it remains relevant and effective. Self-reflection and reassessment, coupled with a well-defined plan, pave the way for a successful and fulfilling career journey.

4

Chapter 4: Skill Development and Lifelong Learning

In today's dynamic job market, continuous skill development is essential for staying competitive. Job loss can be a catalyst for acquiring new skills and enhancing existing ones. This chapter explores various avenues for skill development and the importance of lifelong learning. It emphasizes that investing in education and self-improvement is a powerful strategy for career advancement and personal growth.

The first step in skill development is identifying the skills that are in demand in the desired industry or role. This involves researching job descriptions, industry trends, and employer expectations. Understanding the skills gap helps in prioritizing the areas that need improvement. It ensures that the efforts are focused and aligned with market needs, increasing employability.

Online courses and certifications are valuable resources for skill development. Platforms like Coursera, Udemy, and LinkedIn Learning offer a wide range of courses on various subjects. These courses provide flexibility, allowing individuals to learn at their own pace and convenience. Certifications add credibility to one's resume, showcasing a commitment to professional growth. Investing time and effort in these courses can significantly enhance one's skill set.

Workshops, seminars, and conferences offer opportunities for hands-on learning and networking. Attending industry events provides exposure to new ideas, technologies, and best practices. It also allows individuals to connect with experts and peers, expanding their professional network. Engaging in these activities fosters a culture of continuous learning and keeps individuals updated with the latest developments in their field.

Creating a personal development plan is crucial for staying on track with skill development. This plan should outline specific learning objectives, resources, and timelines. Setting achievable milestones and regularly reviewing progress ensures that the learning goals are met. It also provides a sense of accomplishment and motivation to keep going. Lifelong learning is not just about acquiring new skills; it is about cultivating a mindset of curiosity and growth.

Mentorship and collaboration play a significant role in skill development. Seeking guidance from experienced professionals provides valuable insights and feedback. Collaborating with others on projects or initiatives offers practical experience and knowledge sharing. It creates a supportive environment for learning and growth. Skill development and lifelong learning are continuous processes that require dedication, curiosity, and a proactive approach. By embracing these principles, individuals can navigate the job market with confidence and resilience.

5

Chapter 5: Networking and Building Connections

Networking is a powerful tool for career advancement and job search. Building and maintaining professional relationships can lead to job opportunities, mentorship, and valuable industry insights. This chapter delves into the importance of networking, strategies for effective networking, and tips for building meaningful connections. It emphasizes that networking is not just about finding a job but creating a support system that fosters professional growth.

The foundation of effective networking is building genuine relationships. Authenticity and sincerity are key to connecting with others. It involves showing genuine interest in others' experiences, listening actively, and offering help when possible. Building trust and rapport creates lasting connections that can provide support and guidance throughout one's career.

Expanding one's network requires a proactive approach. Attending industry events, joining professional organizations, and participating in online communities are excellent ways to meet new people. Leveraging social media platforms like LinkedIn allows individuals to connect with professionals across the globe. Engaging in meaningful conversations, sharing insights, and showcasing expertise helps in building a strong online presence.

Informational interviews are a valuable networking strategy. Reaching out to industry professionals for advice and insights provides valuable information and creates new connections. It is an opportunity to learn about different career paths, industry trends, and company cultures. Preparing thoughtful questions and expressing gratitude for the person's time and insights fosters positive relationships.

Giving back to the community is an integral part of networking. Offering help, sharing knowledge, and supporting others creates a culture of reciprocity. Volunteering for industry events, mentoring junior professionals, or participating in collaborative projects are ways to contribute to the community. These actions not only build goodwill but also strengthen one's network and reputation.

Maintaining relationships requires regular effort and follow-up. Staying in Maintaining relationships requires regular effort and follow-up. Staying in touch through periodic check-ins, sharing updates, and expressing gratitude keeps connections alive. It is important to be mindful of maintaining a balance between personal and professional interactions. Building meaningful connections takes time and consistency, but the rewards are worth the investment. A strong network provides support, guidance, and opportunities that can significantly impact one's career journey.

6

Chapter 6: Crafting a Winning Resume and Cover Letter

A well-crafted resume and cover letter are essential tools in a successful job search. These documents serve as the first impression for potential employers and play a crucial role in securing job interviews. This chapter provides detailed guidance on creating compelling and tailored application materials that effectively showcase one's skills, experience, and achievements.

The foundation of an impressive resume is clarity and conciseness. Employers often review resumes quickly, so it is important to present information in a clear and organized manner. This includes using a professional format, concise language, and bullet points to highlight key accomplishments. Tailoring the resume for each job application ensures that it aligns with the specific requirements of the position, increasing the chances of catching the employer's attention.

Showcasing relevant achievements is a key element of a strong resume. Instead of listing job duties, focus on accomplishments that demonstrate the impact of one's work. Using quantifiable metrics, such as percentages, numbers, and specific results, adds credibility and helps employers understand the value brought to previous roles. Including a summary or objective statement at the beginning of the resume provides a brief overview of one's professional profile and career goals.

The cover letter is an opportunity to personalize the application and provide additional context. It should complement the resume by elaborating on key points and highlighting one's enthusiasm for the position. A persuasive cover letter addresses the specific needs of the employer and explains how one's skills and experience align with the job requirements. It should convey a genuine interest in the company and position, making a strong case for why one is the ideal candidate.

Proofreading and seeking feedback are essential steps in the resume and cover letter writing process. Typos, grammatical errors, and inconsistencies can create a negative impression. Taking the time to review and refine these documents ensures that they present a polished and professional image. Additionally, seeking feedback from mentors, career coaches, or peers can provide valuable insights and suggestions for improvement. Crafting a winning resume and cover letter requires attention to detail, strategic thinking, and a commitment to presenting oneself in the best possible light.

7

Chapter 7: Mastering the Job Interview

Job interviews can be nerve-wracking, but with proper preparation, they can also be an opportunity to shine. This chapter provides a comprehensive guide to mastering the job interview process, from researching the company to demonstrating confidence during the interview. By following these strategies, individuals can present themselves as strong candidates and increase their chances of landing their desired job.

The first step in preparing for a job interview is researching the company and the role. Understanding the company's mission, values, products, and recent developments provides valuable context for the interview. This knowledge allows candidates to tailor their responses and demonstrate genuine interest in the organization. It also helps in identifying potential questions and preparing thoughtful answers that align with the company's goals and culture.

Practicing common interview questions is an essential part of interview preparation. Candidates should anticipate questions related to their experience, skills, strengths, weaknesses, and career goals. Preparing concise and compelling responses helps in conveying confidence and clarity during the interview. Additionally, practicing behavioral interview questions using the STAR (Situation, Task, Action, Result) method allows candidates to showcase their problem-solving abilities and accomplishments.

Dressing appropriately for the interview creates a positive first impression.

Candidates should choose professional attire that aligns with the company's dress code. Paying attention to grooming and overall appearance reflects respect and professionalism. A well-presented candidate is more likely to be perceived as confident and competent.

Demonstrating confidence during the interview is crucial for making a strong impression. This includes maintaining good posture, making eye contact, and speaking clearly. Candidates should actively listen to the interviewer's questions and respond thoughtfully. Asking insightful questions about the company and the role shows genuine interest and engagement. It is also important to express enthusiasm for the position and highlight how one's skills and experience make them a good fit.

Following up after the interview is a critical step that many candidates overlook. Sending a thank-you email to the interviewer expresses gratitude for the opportunity and reinforces the candidate's interest in the position. It also provides a chance to reiterate key points from the interview and address any additional questions. A thoughtful follow-up can leave a lasting positive impression and set the candidate apart from other applicants. Mastering the job interview requires preparation, confidence, and effective communication. By following these strategies, individuals can increase their chances of success and move closer to achieving their career goals.

8

Chapter 8: Exploring Alternative Career Paths

J ob loss can be a catalyst for exploring new career paths that align with one's interests and passions. This chapter encourages readers to think outside the box and consider alternative career options, such as freelancing, entrepreneurship, or gig economy work. It discusses the pros and cons of different career paths and provides guidance on how to make a successful transition.

Freelancing offers the flexibility to work on a variety of projects and clients. It allows individuals to leverage their skills and expertise while maintaining control over their schedule and workload. However, freelancing also comes with challenges, such as income instability and the need for self-discipline. To succeed as a freelancer, it is essential to build a strong portfolio, network with potential clients, and manage time effectively. Freelancing can provide a fulfilling and diverse career if approached with the right mindset and strategies.

Entrepreneurship is another alternative career path that offers the opportunity to create and build something from the ground up. Starting a business requires a combination of vision, resilience, and strategic planning. It involves identifying a market need, developing a business plan, securing funding, and executing the plan. While entrepreneurship carries risks, it also offers the potential for significant rewards and personal fulfillment. By pursuing their entrepreneurial ambitions, individuals can turn their passions into profitable ventures.

The gig economy provides a range of opportunities for short-term or project-based work. Platforms like Uber, Airbnb, and Upwork connect individuals with gig opportunities in various industries. The gig economy offers flexibility and the chance to explore different roles and industries. However, it is important to be aware of the lack of job security and benefits associated with gig work. Balancing multiple gigs and managing income can be challenging, but the gig economy can provide valuable experience and income during the transition period.

Exploring alternative career paths also involves considering roles in different industries or sectors. Job loss can be an opportunity to pivot to a new field that aligns with one's interests and values. Conducting informational interviews, researching industry trends, and gaining relevant certifications can facilitate this transition. Being open to new possibilities and willing to learn new skills are key to successfully navigating a career change.

Making a successful transition to an alternative career path requires careful planning and a proactive approach. Setting clear goals, seeking guidance from mentors, and staying adaptable are essential steps. It is important to be patient and persistent, as the journey may involve trial and error. Embracing the uncertainty and viewing it as a learning experience can lead to unexpected and rewarding opportunities. Exploring alternative career paths can open doors to a fulfilling and dynamic professional life.

9

Chapter 9: Financial Management During Transition

Managing finances during a period of unemployment is critical to maintaining stability and reducing stress. This chapter offers practical tips on budgeting, cutting expenses, and seeking financial assistance if needed. It also discusses the importance of building an emergency fund and planning for future financial security. By taking control of their finances, readers can navigate the transition period with greater ease and focus on their job search and career goals without the added burden of financial worries.

The first step in financial management during unemployment is assessing the current financial situation. This involves taking stock of all income, savings, and expenses. Creating a detailed budget helps in understanding where the money is going and identifying areas where costs can be reduced. Prioritizing essential expenses, such as housing, utilities, and groceries, ensures that basic needs are met. Cutting non-essential expenses, such as dining out, subscriptions, and entertainment, can free up funds for more critical needs.

Building an emergency fund is a crucial financial safety net. Ideally, an emergency fund should cover three to six months' worth of living expenses. If one does not already have an emergency fund, it is important to start setting aside money for it as soon as possible. Even small contributions can add up over time. An emergency fund provides a buffer during periods of unemployment and reduces reliance on credit cards or loans, which can lead to debt.

Seeking financial assistance is a viable option during unemployment. Government programs, such as unemployment benefits, food assistance, and housing support, can provide temporary relief. It is important to research and apply for any available assistance programs. Additionally, community organizations and non-profits may offer financial support, job placement services, and counseling. Utilizing these resources can help alleviate financial stress and provide a sense of security.

Exploring alternative income sources can supplement finances during unemployment. Part-time jobs, freelance work, or gig opportunities can provide additional income while searching for a full-time job. Leveraging one's skills and expertise to offer services, such as tutoring, consulting, or crafting, can generate income. It is important to balance these activities with the job search to ensure that enough time and energy are dedicated to finding long-term employment.

Planning for future financial security involves setting long-term financial goals and developing a strategy to achieve them. This includes saving for retirement, investing wisely, and managing debt. Creating a financial plan with the help of a financial advisor can provide guidance and accountability. Building healthy financial habits, such as budgeting, saving, and avoiding unnecessary debt, lays the foundation for a stable and secure financial future. Managing finances during a transition period requires discipline, resourcefulness, and proactive planning. By taking control of their finances, individuals can navigate the challenges of unemployment with confidence and resilience.

10

Chapter 10: Mental and Emotional Well-being

Job loss can have a significant impact on one's mental and emotional well-being. It can trigger feelings of stress, anxiety, and depression, making it essential to prioritize self-care and emotional health during this challenging time. This chapter explores various strategies to maintain mental and emotional well-being, cope with negative emotions, and build resilience in the face of adversity.

Acknowledging and accepting one's emotions is the first step towards emotional healing. It is natural to feel a range of emotions, from sadness and frustration to fear and uncertainty. Allowing oneself to experience and express these emotions, rather than suppressing them, is crucial for emotional recovery. Journaling, talking to trusted friends or family members, or seeking professional counseling can provide a safe outlet for expressing feelings and gaining perspective.

Practicing mindfulness and relaxation techniques can help manage stress and anxiety. Mindfulness involves staying present in the moment and observing one's thoughts and feelings without judgment. Techniques such as deep breathing, meditation, and yoga can promote relaxation and reduce stress levels. Incorporating these practices into daily routines can create a sense of calm and balance, aiding in emotional well-being.

Physical activity is another powerful tool for maintaining mental and emotional health. Regular exercise releases endorphins, which are natural mood boosters. Engaging in physical activities such as walking, running, dancing, or playing sports can improve overall well-being and provide a healthy distraction from negative thoughts. Additionally, maintaining a balanced diet, getting enough sleep, and staying hydrated are essential components of physical and mental health.

Building a support network is vital for emotional resilience. Surrounding oneself with supportive and understanding individuals can provide comfort and encouragement. Joining support groups, either in-person or online, allows for sharing experiences and receiving validation from others who are going through similar challenges. Having a strong support system can foster a sense of belonging and reduce feelings of isolation.

Focusing on positive affirmations and setting realistic goals can also enhance emotional well-being. Positive affirmations involve replacing negative self-talk with encouraging and empowering statements. Setting achievable goals provides a sense of purpose and direction, making it easier to stay motivated and optimistic. Celebrating small accomplishments along the way reinforces a positive outlook and builds confidence. By prioritizing mental and emotional well-being, individuals can navigate the challenges of job loss with greater resilience and emerge stronger on the other side.

11

Chapter 11: Staying Motivated and Persistent

The job search process can be lengthy and challenging, requiring perseverance and determination. Staying motivated and persistent is essential for achieving career goals, even in the face of rejection and setbacks. This chapter offers advice on maintaining motivation, setting realistic goals, and developing strategies to stay focused and resilient throughout the job search journey.

Setting clear and realistic goals provides direction and motivation. Breaking down larger goals into smaller, manageable steps creates a sense of progress and accomplishment. For example, setting daily or weekly targets for job applications, networking activities, or skill development can help maintain momentum. Celebrating small victories along the way reinforces positive behavior and builds confidence.

Creating a structured routine helps in maintaining discipline and focus. Establishing a daily schedule that includes specific times for job search activities, skill development, and self-care ensures that all aspects of the job search are addressed. A routine provides stability and a sense of purpose, reducing feelings of aimlessness. It also helps in managing time effectively and preventing burnout.

Staying positive and maintaining a growth mindset is crucial for motivation.

Embracing challenges as opportunities for learning and growth fosters resilience. Instead of viewing rejection as a failure, it is helpful to see it as a chance to refine one's approach and improve. Seeking feedback from interviews and using it constructively can enhance future performance. Believing in one's abilities and staying optimistic about the future are key components of a growth mindset.

Seeking inspiration and staying connected with positive influences can boost motivation. Reading success stories, listening to motivational podcasts, or engaging with uplifting content can provide encouragement. Surrounding oneself with supportive and positive individuals fosters a motivating environment. Sharing experiences and seeking advice from mentors, peers, or support groups can provide valuable insights and encouragement.

Practicing self-compassion and avoiding self-criticism is essential for maintaining motivation. It is important to recognize that the job search process can be challenging and that setbacks are a normal part of the journey. Being kind to oneself, acknowledging efforts, and focusing on progress rather than perfection can reduce stress and enhance motivation. By staying motivated and persistent, individuals can navigate the job search journey with resilience and ultimately achieve their career aspirations.

12

Chapter 12: Celebrating Success and Moving Forward

The journey from job loss to success is filled with challenges and growth opportunities. Celebrating successes, no matter how small, is an important part of this journey. It reinforces positive behavior, builds confidence, and provides motivation for future endeavors. This chapter focuses on recognizing and celebrating achievements, reflecting on the journey, and setting new goals for continued growth and success.

Recognizing and celebrating achievements involves acknowledging the effort and progress made during the job search journey. Whether it's securing a job interview, completing a certification, or networking with industry professionals, each milestone deserves recognition. Celebrating successes reinforces a positive mindset and provides a sense of accomplishment. It is important to take the time to reflect on these achievements and appreciate the hard work and dedication that led to them.

Reflecting on the journey allows for valuable insights and personal growth. It provides an opportunity to evaluate what worked well and what could be improved. Reflecting on challenges and how they were overcome fosters a sense of resilience and adaptability. It also highlights strengths and areas for further development. This reflection is essential for continued growth and success in one's career.

Setting new goals ensures that the momentum of growth continues. It is important to keep pushing forward and striving for new heights. Setting both short-term and long-term goals provides direction and motivation. Short-term goals focus on immediate actions and achievements, while long-term goals provide a vision for the future. Revisiting and adjusting these goals regularly ensures that they remain relevant and aligned with personal and professional aspirations.

Embracing a mindset of lifelong learning and personal development is key to sustained success. The job market is constantly evolving, and staying updated with industry trends and skills is essential. Pursuing new learning opportunities, seeking mentorship, and staying curious fosters continuous growth. Embracing challenges and being open to change ensures that one remains adaptable and resilient in the face of future uncertainties.

Moving forward with confidence and optimism is the final step in shaping success post-job loss. The journey may have been challenging, but it has also been an opportunity for growth and transformation. By celebrating successes, reflecting on the journey, and setting new goals, individuals can continue to thrive and achieve their career aspirations. The experience of job loss, though difficult, can ultimately lead to a more fulfilling and successful professional life.

Book Description: Shaping Success, Post-Job Loss

In "Shaping Success, Post-Job Loss," embark on a transformative journey of resilience, self-discovery, and triumph. This empowering guide offers practical strategies, heartfelt encouragement, and inspiring stories to help readers navigate the challenging aftermath of job loss and emerge stronger than ever.

From the initial shock and emotional turmoil to embracing change and exploring new career paths, each chapter provides valuable insights and actionable steps to turn adversity into opportunity. Through self-reflection, skill development, and effective networking, readers will uncover their true potential and reshape their professional lives with confidence and purpose.

"Shaping Success, Post-Job Loss" delves into essential topics such as financial management during transition, maintaining mental and emotional well-being, and mastering the job interview process. With a focus on lifelong learning, continuous growth, and celebrating small victories, this book is a comprehensive roadmap for those determined to reclaim their success and build a fulfilling career.

Whether you're facing unemployment or seeking to support someone who is, this book is a beacon of hope and a testament to the indomitable human spirit. Embrace the journey, harness your resilience, and shape your success—one step at a time.

www.ingramcontent.com/pod-product-compliance
Lightning Source LLC
LaVergne TN
LVHW020743090526
838202LV00057BA/6214